AF228543

BROOKLYN NETS

BY BRIAN MAHONEY

SportsZone

An Imprint of Abdo Publishing
abdobooks.com

abdobooks.com

Published by Abdo Publishing, a division of ABDO, PO Box 398166, Minneapolis, Minnesota 55439. Copyright © 2023 by Abdo Consulting Group, Inc. International copyrights reserved in all countries. No part of this book may be reproduced in any form without written permission from the publisher. SportsZone™ is a trademark and logo of Abdo Publishing.

Printed in China
052022
092022

Cover Photo: Noah K. Murray/AP Images
Interior Photos: Melinda Nagy/Shutterstock Images, 1; Kathy Willens/AP Images, 4, 10, 19; Jim McIsaac/Getty Images Sport/Getty Images, 6; Corey Sipkin/AP Images, 8; Focus On Sport/Getty Images, 12, 15; John Lent/AP Images, 14; Ron Frehm/AP Images, 17; Maddie Malhotra/Getty Images Sport/Getty Images, 20; Ross Lewis/Getty Images Sport/Getty Images, 22; Gary Stewart/AP Images, 25; Bill Kostroun/AP Images, 27; John Minchillo/AP Images, 29; Al Bello/Getty Images Sport/Getty Images, 30; Focus On Sport/Getty Images Sport/Getty Images, 32, 36; Richard Drew/AP Images, 35; Gary Dineen/NBAE/Getty Images, 38; Elsa/Getty Images Sport/Getty Images, 41

Editor: Charlie Beattie
Series Designer: Joshua Olson

Library of Congress Control Number: 2021951669

Publisher's Cataloging-in-Publication Data

Names: Mahoney, Brian, author.
Title: Brooklyn Nets / by Brian Mahoney
Description: Minneapolis, Minnesota: Abdo Publishing, 2023 | Series: Inside the NBA | Includes online resources and index.
Identifiers: ISBN 9781532198205 (lib. bdg.) | ISBN 9781098271855 (ebook)
Subjects: LCSH: Brooklyn Nets (Basketball team)--Juvenile literature. | Basketball--Juvenile literature. | Professional sports--Juvenile literature. | Sports franchises--Juvenile literature.
Classification: DDC 796.32364--dc23

TABLE OF
CONTENTS

TOMORROW
MIDDLETON
22
BKLYN
NETS
7
NETS
BROOK
NEW
SPALDING
4

CHAPTER ONE

DURANT DOES IT ALL

Kevin Durant knew the Brooklyn Nets were going to need him more than ever. Game 5 of the team's 2021 Eastern Conference semifinal series against the Milwaukee Bucks was Brooklyn's most important game of the season. The series was tied 2–2. The Nets were playing at home. They didn't want to go back to Milwaukee facing elimination.

However, in a huge moment, the Nets had come out flat. Brooklyn was losing by 16 points when it went back to its locker room at halftime. The Nets had scored only 43 points. The performance was a huge letdown for a team that had averaged nearly 120 per game in the regular season. Durant had six of the team's 14 baskets. If Brooklyn was going to come back to win, the star power forward knew he would need an even bigger second-half performance.

Kevin Durant averaged 34.3 points per game during Brooklyn's 2021 playoff run.

Before joining the Nets, Durant was a two-time NBA Finals MVP for the Golden State Warriors.

BETTER THAN EVER

When the 2020–21 season began, Durant had not played in more than a year. He had ruptured his Achilles tendon, located at the back of the lower leg, while playing for the Golden State Warriors in the 2019 National Basketball Association (NBA) Finals. Durant needed surgery to repair the injury. Shortly after his injury, he decided to leave Golden State and go to Brooklyn.

But he was not able to play during the 2019–20 season. Many wondered what he would be like after he returned.

The 10-time All-Star and former league Most Valuable Player (MVP) ended up playing as well as ever. He scored at least 20 points in each of his first 17 games as a Net. Though Durant missed several games down the stretch with a hamstring injury, he shone whenever he was in the lineup. In 35 games, he averaged 26.9 points per contest.

"The injuries that he's been through, to come back even from the Achilles to the hamstring to get back in this position, the world is witnessing, once again, who is the best player in the world," Nets teammate Jeff Green said.

MORE THAN A SCORER

Durant's scoring ability was never a secret. The skinny 6-foot-10 big man had led the NBA in points per game four times entering the 2020–21 season. He averaged 32.6 points in the Nets' first-round series win against the Boston Celtics. That was the highest ever for a Nets player in a playoff series. However, because he was such a great scorer, the rest of his game didn't get much attention. But against Milwaukee, his all-around production was hard to miss. Durant had double-doubles of points and rebounds in three of the first four games of the series.

The Nets hoped the trio of James Harden, *left*, Durant, *center*, and Kyrie Irving, *right*, would make them a title contender in 2021.

Heading into Game 5, the Nets were hobbling. Guard James Harden had hurt his hamstring in Game 1 of the series and was just getting back to action. Point guard Kyrie Irving was out after spraining his ankle in Game 4.

At halftime of Game 5, the Bucks were cruising toward a third consecutive win. They started hot. Though Durant had made the first basket of the game, the Bucks scored the next 12 points. Milwaukee held that double-digit lead through most of the first half. At the break, the Bucks led 59–43. Meanwhile, Harden was struggling on his injured leg. He missed all six of his shots in the first half. Durant needed to be the hero if Brooklyn had a chance to come back.

TRIPLE THREAT

Nearing the halfway point of the third quarter, the Nets hadn't made a dent in Milwaukee's lead. The score stood 76–60 in favor of the Bucks. Then Durant turned it on. He made his first basket of the second half on a layup with 6:18 left in the third quarter. With 4:09 left, Milwaukee's lead had been shaved to 77–70.

Durant was far from done. With 31 seconds left in the quarter, he drove to his right. Durant gained a quick step on Bucks forward P. J. Tucker. Milwaukee center Brook Lopez came over to help. As Durant threw up a high shot over the 7-foot Lopez, Tucker fouled Durant. As the whistle blew, the ball banked in off the glass.

The Nets scored 38 points in the third quarter. Durant had 11 of them. But he also grabbed six rebounds and added five assists. It was hard to imagine a player could do more to win a game. Yet in the fourth quarter, Durant took it to another level.

FANTASTIC FOURTH

Through three quarters of play, Durant had played all 36 minutes. That was already higher than his season average for a full game. But he still showed plenty of energy. As the Nets continued to dig into Milwaukee's lead, Durant did

Best of the Nets

Kevin Durant scored at least 40 points three times in the 2020–21 playoffs. In their entire NBA history, the Nets had only three other 40-point performances in postseason games. James Harden, guard Vince Carter, and forward Dražen Petrović each did it once.

Durant savors the moment after knocking down a three-pointer in the fourth quarter of Game 5 against Milwaukee.

what he was best known for. He scored Brooklyn's first two baskets of the quarter. With 8:36 left he drilled a three-pointer to give the Nets a 94–93 lead. The crowd erupted at Brooklyn's first lead since the game's opening minute.

The advantage didn't last long. Milwaukee forward Khris Middleton answered with a three-pointer of his own. But Durant shrugged off the setback. He came around a screen set by point guard Bruce Brown and drilled a shot from 27 feet.

For the rest of the quarter, the Nets fought off every attack by the Bucks. Brooklyn never trailed again. But Milwaukee did cut the lead to 106–105 with 1:14 left. It was time for Durant to put the game away.

On Brooklyn's next possession, the shot clock was running down. Two Bucks defenders were swarming Harden 30 feet from the basket. Durant came over to help, then peeled away, taking Middleton with him. Harden flipped a lob pass over Middleton's head and into Durant's arms. Durant then flipped up a three-pointer just before the shot-clock buzzer sounded. As the shot rattled in, Durant posed for the roaring Brooklyn crowd.

By now, Durant already had a triple-double. No matter what happened next, it was one of the best playoff performances in NBA history. But he still had one more trick to pull. Milwaukee pulled to within two points and had a possession to tie it with 15 seconds left. Middleton drove the lane but at the last second dished off to Giannis Antetokounmpo. The ball bounced off the Milwaukee star's hands. Durant swooped in and snatched it up. After a foul, Durant made two free throws to complete the victory.

The final score was 114–108 in favor of the Nets. Durant's final stat line read 49 points, 17 rebounds, 10 assists, three steals, and two blocked shots. No one had ever scored at least 45 points, grabbed 15 rebounds, and handed out 10 assists in an NBA playoff game. He scored 31 of his points in the second half and 20 in the fourth quarter alone.

After the game, Nets coach Steve Nash summed up his star forward's play in just three words. "Historic, historic performance," Nash said.

NETS
32

CHAPTER TWO

NOMADIC NETS

The Nets have called the New York/New Jersey area home for the franchise's entire existence. But for a team that hasn't moved far, the Nets have roamed quite a bit. The team has changed arenas, states, hometowns, nicknames, and even leagues.

In Brooklyn, the Nets play in Barclays Center, one of the NBA's newest and nicest arenas. It is the eighth arena the Nets have called home since they started playing in 1967.

It opened in 2012 and cost roughly $1 billion to build. It sits in a busy plaza, surrounded by stores, restaurants, and one of the biggest subway stations in New York City. But it took many years of struggling in much smaller buildings in smaller cities before the Nets found such a glamorous home.

In the mid-1960s, a new basketball league was starting up to rival the NBA. The American Basketball Association (ABA)

Thanks to stars like Julius Erving, the Nets were a powerhouse in the ABA.

Forward Rick Barry grabs a rebound during a Nets game in 1970.

was founded in 1967. The New York Americans were set to be one of the league's first franchises. Team owner Arthur Brown secured them a home arena at the 69th Regiment Armory in Manhattan.

There was only one problem. New York already had an NBA team playing in Manhattan. The New York Knicks were not too happy with another professional basketball team starting on their turf. The Knicks pressured the Armory to back out of hosting the Americans.

Brown was forced to find a new home for the team and located one just across the Hudson River in Teaneck, New Jersey. Now called the New Jersey Americans, the team played its first season there.

The next year, Brown found a new home back in New York. The Nets spent the next nine years playing in three different arenas on Long Island, just east of New York City. And they changed their name to the New York Nets.

Erving (32) averaged 28.2 points per game during his three seasons with the Nets.

DYNASTY YEARS

It was on Long Island that the Nets blossomed into one of the ABA's best teams. From 1969–70 to 1975–76, the Nets made the playoffs every season. In 1973 New York added forward Julius Erving from the rival Virginia Squires. By far the league's best player, Erving led the Nets to ABA championships in 1974 and 1976.

The Nets were poised to become a dynasty. Erving was only 25 years old. Star guards Brian Taylor and John Williamson were only 24. But big changes were coming to the Nets and the league they played in.

SWITCHING LEAGUES, SWITCHING STATES

The Nets' 1976 championship marked the end of the ABA era. The league merged with the NBA that summer. Four ABA teams, including the Nets, moved over to the NBA. Once again this caused a problem with the Knicks. New York's established NBA team thought the Nets were invading their home territory. The league forced the Nets to pay the Knicks nearly $5 million to stay in New York.

With that money gone, Nets owner Roy Boe could not afford to give Erving a raise. Boe was forced to sell the star forward's contract to the Philadelphia 76ers. Instead of the Nets joining the NBA as a powerhouse, they were one of the worst teams in their new league. The Nets finished 22–60.

The next season, the Nets were on the move again. They went back across the Hudson River and relocated in New Jersey. With the move came a new name once again. The team was now the New Jersey Nets.

The Nets played four seasons at Rutgers University while a new arena was built in an area called the Meadowlands in East

Rutherford, New Jersey, which is near New York City. During that stretch, the team struggled. In their first five NBA seasons, the Nets made the playoffs only once.

Things finally began to turn around for the Nets in the 1981–82 season. Under Hall of Fame coach Larry Brown, the Nets went 44–38. It was their first winning record in the NBA. Better yet, they moved to East Rutherford, where the new Brendan Byrne Arena gave them a permanent home.

Buck Williams throws down a dunk against the Knicks during a game in 1987.

They stayed in the arena for nearly three decades. New Jersey finished fourth in the league in attendance and hosted the 1982 NBA All-Star Game.

Led by players such as Buck Williams, Darryl Dawkins, Micheal Ray Richardson, and Otis Birdsong, the Nets made the playoffs in five straight seasons. Their first series victory was a stunner. The Nets knocked off the defending NBA champion 76ers in 1984.

BACK-TO-BACK

That success did not last. By 1986–87 the Nets were back in the NBA basement. The Nets continued to stumble through the 1990s. While the neighboring Knicks were a contender, New Jersey was a laughingstock. The Nets made the playoffs four times but never won a single round.

New Jersey's big breakthrough finally came in 2001. The Nets traded for point guard Jason Kidd. The versatile playmaker led them to the NBA Finals in 2002 and 2003. Though they lost both series, the Nets had crawled out of the Knicks' shadow for the first time. New Jersey won four Atlantic Division titles in five years and made six playoff appearances in a row. That was the team's longest streak since it had been in the ABA.

Kidd was traded in 2008. The Nets couldn't maintain their success. The 2009–10 season was the last at the East Rutherford arena, which had been renamed the Izod Center. The team finished 12–70.

Swamped

In 1994 the Nets were considering a name change. Team president Jon Spoelstra didn't like "Nets" as a nickname. The team's arena at the time was built in a former swamp called the Meadowlands. Spoelstra dreamed up the nickname "Swamp Dragons." The league approved the name change, but the idea died when Nets co-owner David Gerstein voted against it.

Guard Deron Williams, *front*, was an All-Star twice during his five seasons playing for the Nets.

BROOKLYN BOUND

By 2010 there had been rumors that the Nets would move back to New York City for several years. Owner Bruce Ratner wanted the team to settle in the borough of Brooklyn. Now Ratner

Kyrie Irving, *left*, joined the Nets one day before Kevin Durant, *right*, was signed in the summer of 2019.

had a new arena being built, Barclays Center. The team played in Newark, New Jersey, for two seasons until construction was completed.

By the time the Nets landed in Brooklyn, they had another new owner. Mikhail Prokhorov, a billionaire from Russia, bought most of team from Ratner. He set a goal of winning the NBA championship within five years. Over the next few years, the now Brooklyn Nets traded for star players such as guards Deron Williams and Joe Johnson and forwards Kevin Garnett and Paul Pierce. The moves got the team to the playoffs during its first three years in Brooklyn. But the Nets never got close to the Finals.

By the 2019–20 season, the Nets were a losing team. But they started making big noise before the year began. The team had another new owner, Taiwanese businessman Joseph Tsai. They also added two of the NBA's biggest stars. Point guard Kyrie Irving signed as a free agent on July 6, 2019. The next day, forward Kevin Durant came to the team in a deal with the Golden State Warriors.

Durant couldn't play for the Nets that year as he was recovering from a torn Achilles tendon. But Irving helped lead Brooklyn to the playoffs. In January 2021, another star guard came on board. High-scoring James Harden was acquired from the Houston Rockets. The three stars took Brooklyn back to the postseason in 2021, but their time together was short. Harden was traded to the Philadelphia 76ers in February 2022 as the Nets continued to seek the right combination of players to make them champions.

CHAPTER THREE

NIFTY NETS

In 1972 the New York Nets went to the ABA Finals. The team was led by high-scoring forward Rick Barry, who averaged 31.5 points per game that season. But the next year, Barry went back to the NBA. The Nets struggled without a star and finished the 1972–73 season 30–54.

Luckily for New York, the Virginia Squires were losing money. They needed cash to keep going. The Squires also had a star player in Julius Erving. The Nets threw $750,000 at the Squires and brought Erving to the Big Apple.

Erving was by far the brightest light in the ABA. He had a smooth, effortless style that poured in one graceful-looking basket after another. He also had a cool nickname. Erving was known simply as "Dr. J."

Erving helped popularize the dunk. And he did it with style. That was on display when he won the ABA's slam dunk

Julius Erving earned his iconic nickname, "Dr. J," from a high school friend in Roosevelt, New York.

contest in 1976. On his most famous slam, he took off from the free-throw line. However, dunking was just one of his talents. Former NBA coach Johnny Kerr referred to Erving as "Thomas Edison." Kerr said it was because "he invents something new every night."

Erving led the Nets to two ABA championships in his three years with the team. He was the MVP of the league all three of those seasons. Erving averaged 29.3 points during the ABA's final season in 1975–76. That led the league in scoring.

That was the last season of the ABA. Unfortunately for the Nets, it was also their last season with Erving. They couldn't agree to a contract with Erving as they made the jump into the NBA. They eventually sent him to the Philadelphia 76ers in exchange for $3 million just before the 1976–77 season was set to begin. Erving went on to succeed with the 76ers. But the Nets struggled without him.

Dr. J to the Knicks?

The Nets were forced to move Julius Erving to the 76ers to cover heavy fees they owed to the New York Knicks in order to join the NBA. The Knicks charged the Nets nearly $5 million for "invading" the Knicks' territory. Nets owner Roy Boe offered to give the Knicks Erving instead of paying the fee. But the Knicks turned down the move. Knicks fans can only look back now and wonder, *what if?*

POWER POSTS

The Nets drafted their next scoring star, forward Bernard King, in the summer of 1977.

He spent two amazing seasons with the Nets, averaging more than 21 points each year. But King was traded to the Utah Jazz before the 1979–80 season.

A year later, the Nets used the third overall pick on power forward Buck Williams. Like King, he made an instant impact. Williams was an All-Star during his rookie season in 1981–82. It was the first time since joining the NBA that a Nets player was selected.

Buck Williams (52) blocks a shot attempt from Seattle SuperSonics forward Xavier McDaniel in 1989.

Unlike Erving and King, Williams was not a flashy player. The 6-foot-8-inch, 215-pound forward was a decent scorer. But he was one of the league's best rebounders. Williams averaged a double-double in his first seven NBA seasons. Along with center Darryl Dawkins and guards Otis Birdsong and Micheal Ray Richardson, Williams was a huge part of the Nets' 1984 playoff team. That year the Nets upset Erving's 76ers to win their first NBA playoff series.

A decade after Williams debuted, New Jersey picked up another rookie power forward. Derrick Coleman was the top pick in the 1990 draft out of Syracuse University. He looked like a star from day one. Coleman won Rookie of the Year honors in 1991.

Playing with point guard Kenny Anderson and shooting guard Dražen Petrović, Coleman helped the Nets get back to the playoffs in 1992 and 1993. Those teams were coached by NBA legend Chuck Daly, who had just won two titles with the Detroit Pistons. Daly had also coached the 1992 US Olympic "Dream Team" at the Games in Barcelona, Spain.

Daly's Nets had promise, but they did not win a playoff round either year. Coleman never reached the potential he showed as a rookie, as injuries hampered his career. The Nets traded him to Philadelphia in 1995.

Tragedy Strikes

Guard Dražen Petrović came to the Nets in a trade with the Portland Trail Blazers in 1991. By the end of the 1992–93 season, the Croatian player was emerging as one of the NBA's best shooters. That year he averaged 22.3 points per game. However, his life was cut short that summer. Petrović's car collided with a stalled semitruck on a highway in Germany. He was 28 years old.

NEW KIDD IN TOWN

In 2001 the Nets had an All-Star point guard in Stephon Marbury. He was also a local from the Coney Island neighborhood of Brooklyn. But Marbury's

Jason Kidd, *left*, helped the Nets reach the NBA Finals twice after joining the team in 2001.

main skill was scoring. He had averaged more than 23 points per game the season before, but the Nets finished 26–56. In July the Nets made a deal with the Phoenix Suns. As part of a five-player trade, they swapped point guards. The Nets received Jason Kidd. The 28-year-old Kidd was Marbury's exact opposite. Though not an elite scorer, he was an amazing passer and defender, as well as a solid rebounder.

Kidd turned the Nets around immediately. Alongside scoring forwards Keith Van Horn and Kenyon Martin and guard Kerry Kittles, Kidd's 2001–02 Nets improved by 26 wins to 52. Then they knocked out the Indiana Pacers, Charlotte Hornets, and Boston Celtics on their way to the NBA Finals. Kidd was the runner-up for the 2002 NBA MVP Award.

Kidd scored a career-high 18.7 points per game the next season but still led the NBA in assists. The Nets made a return trip to the Finals. Kidd stayed with the team until a midseason trade in 2008. Along with athletic forwards Vince Carter and Richard Jefferson in the later years, Kidd's Nets were a consistent playoff presence.

BALLING IN BROOKLYN

The Nets needed a star player to attract fans for their move to Brooklyn. They spent much of the 2010–11 season trying to arrange a trade with the Denver Nuggets for All-Star Carmelo Anthony. But when the Nuggets instead sent Anthony to the New York Knicks that February, the Nets moved on. The next day they traded for Utah Jazz point guard Deron Williams.

Williams paired with Joe Johnson in what the Nets nicknamed "Brooklyn's Backcourt." Then the Nets worked out a huge trade with Boston in 2013, getting veteran forwards Kevin Garnett and Paul Pierce. With those four players joining center Brook Lopez, the Nets appeared to have one of the best

Nets guard Joe Johnson celebrates after hitting a buzzer-beater against the Detroit Pistons in 2012.

starting fives in the NBA. They also had Kidd back. The recently retired point guard signed on as the Nets' new head coach.

The Nets made the second round of the playoffs in 2014. But Kidd then left to coach the Milwaukee Bucks, and Pierce signed with the Washington Wizards. The rest of the core was gone within two years.

However, that rebuild got a major boost over a two-day span in July 2019. That summer Kevin Durant was a free agent. He had been playing with the powerhouse Golden State Warriors, where he won two NBA titles. On July 7,

Kevin Durant had not played in over a year when he finally suited up for the Nets in December 2020, but he still averaged 26.9 points per game that season.

Durant announced he was planning to sign with the Nets. The 6-foot-10-inch forward who could both slash to the basket and hit three-pointers was coming to Brooklyn. The Nets now had one of the NBA's best-ever scorers on board.

It was the second big move of the month for Brooklyn. The day before, former Celtics point guard Kyrie Irving had signed as a free agent as well. With Irving's quickness and passing skills combined with Durant's scoring, the Nets were ready to improve.

They had to wait a year to play together while Durant recovered from an Achilles injury suffered in the 2019 NBA Finals. But the two suited up together for the first time in December 2020. The COVID-19 pandemic had delayed the start of the season. But it was worth the wait. The duo combined for 48 points while routing Golden State 125–99.

The Nets thought they were adding another key piece a month later when former NBA MVP James Harden came over from the Houston Rockets. But Harden, Irving, and Durant hardly ever played together. During their time together on the roster, the trio only ever appeared in the same game 16 times. Harden was dealt to the Philadelphia 76ers in February 2022. The Nets continued to pin their future on Durant.

CHAPTER FOUR

NETS MEMORIES

While the NBA was an established league, the ABA was wild in its early days. The New Jersey Americans' first trip to the playoffs was another example of why.

In the spring of 1967, both the Americans and the Kentucky Colonels finished 36–42. With only one playoff spot left to grab, the teams needed a one-game playoff to decide things. The game was supposed to be played in New Jersey. But there was one problem—the Americans' arena was hosting a circus on the same day.

New Jersey scrambled to find a place to play the game before settling on Long Island Arena in Commack, New York. But when the teams arrived to play, they found a gym that was not ready to host a game. Among other things, the floorboards were loose.

Nets center Billy Paultz attempts a jump shot against the Indiana Pacers in 1972.

ABA commissioner George Mikan ordered both teams to head to Bloomington, Minnesota, and play there. Then he changed his mind and ordered the Americans to forfeit, because their home stadium had been unavailable. But there was a happy ending for the Americans. They cleaned up Long Island Arena and made it their home the next season as the New York Nets.

LEAVING ON TOP

In 1974 the Nets won their first ABA championship. Led by head coach Kevin Loughery and star Julius Erving, the Nets lost only two games in three playoff rounds. They routed the Utah Stars 4–1 to claim the title.

Two years later, the ABA was ready to fold. But the league still played one final season. The Nets made it back to the Finals to face the Denver Nuggets. Both teams were headed for the NBA when the series was over. But who would leave the ABA as a champion?

Erving offered up an answer by scoring 45 points in a 120–118 Game 1 victory. His final two points came on a game-winning baseline jump shot in the final second. However, Denver rallied to win Game 2. The Nets then won two of the next three and entered Game 6 with a chance to claim a championship on their home floor.

The Nets celebrate after winning Game 6 of the 1976 ABA Finals over the Denver Nuggets, the last game in the league's history.

The Nuggets came out rolling. Behind star forward David Thompson and guard Dan Issel, Denver built a 22-point third-quarter lead. However, the Nets still had Erving, the league MVP. He joined up with guard John Williamson to lead an epic comeback. The Nets rallied, outscoring the Nuggets 34–14 in the game's final quarter. Williamson had 24 points in the second half. Erving finished the series with a 31-point, 19-rebound effort. It was his final game as a Net, and he made sure the team left the ABA at the top of the heap.

STUNNING THE SIXERS

Erving was on the other side of the court when the Nets finally made a playoff memory in the NBA. In 1984 his Philadelphia 76ers were defending NBA champions. His old team still had not won a playoff game in the league.

Guard Micheal Ray Richardson, *right*, averaged 16.8 points and a team-high 7.2 assists during the Nets playoff run in 1984.

The first round of the 1984 Eastern Conference playoffs between the teams looked like a mismatch. But the Nets shocked everyone by winning Game 1 116–101 in Philadelphia. Nets forward Buck Williams led the way with 25 points and 16 rebounds.

In Game 2 New Jersey guard Micheal Ray Richardson's 32 points stole the show. The Nets won again, this time 116–102. In the best-of-five series, the underdogs had the 76ers in big trouble. However, Philadelphia won both games in New Jersey. Game 5 came back to the 76ers' home floor. Erving said there was no way the Nets would win there again. The Nets took Dr. J's prediction as motivation. They held Erving to 12 points. Still, it looked over late in the game when the 76ers had a 90–83 fourth-quarter lead. But the Nets rallied for a 101–98 victory.

"That was a great experience," New Jersey's Albert King said. "You were going up against the NBA champions. No one gave you a chance when you were starting on their court."

FINALLY, THE FINALS

The upset of Philadelphia in 1984 remained the Nets' only NBA playoff series victory entering the 2002 postseason. Three series later, the Nets were in the NBA Finals.

The Nets had won 52 games in 2001–02, their best total yet in the NBA. After beating the Indiana Pacers and Charlotte Hornets, the Nets played the Boston Celtics in the Eastern Conference finals. New Jersey took a 3–2 lead into Game 6. But once again, the Nets needed to rally. Jason Kidd's triple-double helped the Nets overcome a 54–44 halftime deficit. With 50 seconds left in the fourth

Frank's Fast Start

The Nets fired Byron Scott during the 2003–04 season. They could not have imagined a better start under their next coach. New Jersey won its first 13 games after Lawrence Frank took over on January 26, 2004. That gave Frank the longest winning streak by an NBA coach to start his career.

Guard Joe Johnson was with the Nets when they moved to Brooklyn in 2012–13 and was an All-Star the next year.

quarter, forward Keith Van Horn's three-pointer put the game out of reach for Boston in a 96–88 victory. Kidd averaged 17.5 points, 11.2 rebounds, and 10.2 assists in the series.

The dream run ended there. The Los Angeles Lakers overmatched New Jersey in the NBA Finals with a four-game sweep. The Nets were back in the Finals again a year later, this time facing the San Antonio Spurs. Kidd's 30 points led the way for New Jersey's first ever Finals game victory, 87–85, in Game 2. The teams split the first four games, but San Antonio won Games 5 and 6 to claim the trophy.

BROOK-LYN! BROOK-LYN!

The Nets were scheduled to begin the Brooklyn era against the New York Knicks on November 1, 2012. But three days earlier, New York was damaged by Hurricane Sandy. New York City mayor Michael Bloomberg requested the game be postponed.

Instead, the Nets opened against the Toronto Raptors on November 3. When they took the floor at the new Barclays Center to start the game, they became Brooklyn's first major professional sports team since baseball's Dodgers moved to Los Angeles after the 1957 season.

It was clear how excited Brooklyn fans were to have a team of their own again. Fans loudly chanted "Brook-lyn! Brook-lyn!" near the end of the Nets' 107–100 victory.

"That gave me jitters, man. Chills," guard Joe Johnson said.

NEARLY SEVENTH HEAVEN

Kevin Durant was not done making playoff history after his triple-double in Game 5 of the 2021 playoffs against the Milwaukee Bucks. Four days later, the two teams were back in Brooklyn for Game 7.

Durant came out firing, and his 20 first-half points helped Brooklyn build a six-point halftime lead. But Milwaukee's Giannis Antetokounmpo rallied the Bucks in the second half. With 2:32 left, the Bucks led 104–101. But Durant answered. He scored the Nets' next three baskets and kept his team in the game.

With six seconds left, the Nets forced a turnover. They got the ball back down 109–107. Jeff Green inbounded from the sideline. He flung a cross-court pass to Durant, who squared up to his defender. After backing his man down just inside the three-point line, Durant spun to his right and hoisted a long jump shot. As it dropped in, the fans in Brooklyn's Barclays Center erupted. Only one second showed on the clock.

The only question was, had Durant tied the game or had he won it? His foot was very close to the three-point line. After an official review, it was determined his size-18 shoe had just touched the stripe. The game was going to overtime.

In the extra session, the Nets ran out of gas. They scored only two points as Milwaukee held on for a 115–111 victory.

Kevin Durant, *right*, shoots over Milwaukee's P. J. Tucker to force overtime in Game 7 of the teams' 2021 playoff matchup.

The Bucks went on to win the NBA title a month later. But Durant's 48 points set a record for the most scored in a Game 7. He proved once again that as long as "K. D." was on the floor, the Nets had a chance to be great.

TIMELINE

1967

The New Jersey Americans play their first season in the ABA, playing home games in Teaneck, New Jersey.

1968

The team moves to Commack, on Long Island, and becomes the New York Nets.

1969

The Nets move again, this time to West Hempstead, New York, and make their first playoff appearance after the 1969–70 season.

1972

The Nets move into the Nassau Veterans Memorial Coliseum in Uniondale, New York. They go on to reach the ABA championship series before losing to the Indiana Pacers.

1974

Julius Erving is voted ABA MVP and leads New York to its first championship.

1976

In the final season of the ABA, the Nets win their second title and Erving wins his third straight MVP Award. The Nets then move to the NBA but lose Erving to the Philadelphia 76ers before the 1976–77 season begins.

1977

The Nets move back to New Jersey and become the New Jersey Nets.

1981

The Nets move to East Rutherford, New Jersey, where they will spend the next 29 years.

1984

The Nets win an NBA playoff series for the first time by knocking off the defending champion 76ers.

1991

Derrick Coleman is voted Rookie of the Year after averaging 18.4 points and 10.3 rebounds per game.

1993

The Nets make the playoffs under Chuck Daly, but leading scorer Dražen Petrović dies in a car accident after the season.

2001

Jason Kidd is acquired by the Nets and leads them to their first NBA Finals after the 2001–02 season. However, they fall to the Los Angeles Lakers.

2003

The Nets reach the NBA Finals for the second straight season but lose to the San Antonio Spurs in six games.

2009

The Nets set an NBA record by losing their first 18 games of the season and finish 12–70.

2012

The Nets begin playing in Brooklyn as the Brooklyn Nets.

2019

The Nets sign All-Stars Kevin Durant and Kyrie Irving.

2020

Brooklyn hires Steve Nash as head coach. The former NBA point guard leads the Nets to the second round of the playoffs in his first season.

FRANCHISE HISTORY
New Jersey Americans
(1967–68)
New York Nets (1968–77)
New Jersey Nets (1977–2012)
Brooklyn Nets (2012–)

ABA CHAMPIONSHIPS
1974, 1976

KEY PLAYERS
Kenny Anderson (1991–96)
Vince Carter (2004–09)
Derrick Coleman (1990–95)
Kevin Durant (2019–)
Julius Erving (1973–76)
Kyrie Irving (2019–)
Richard Jefferson (2001–08)
Jason Kidd (2001–08)
Kenyon Martin (2000–04)
Keith Van Horn (1997–2002)
Buck Williams (1981–89)
Deron Williams (2011–15)
John Williamson (1973–77,
1978–80)

KEY COACHES
Kevin Loughery (1973–80)
Steve Nash (2020–)
Byron Scott (2000–04)

HOME ARENAS
Teaneck Armory (1967–68)
Long Island Arena (1968–69)
Island Garden (1969–72)
Nassau Coliseum (1972–77)
Rutgers Athletic Center
(1977–81)
Izod Center (1981–2010)
Known as:
Brendan Byrne Arena
(1981–96)
Continental Airlines Arena
(1996–2007)
Prudential Center (2010–12)
Barclays Center (2012–)

MUSIC ROYALTY

Husband-and-wife entertainers Jay-Z and Beyoncé were at the Nets' first game in Brooklyn. Jay-Z owned a small portion of the team at the time.

WAITING FOR A WIN

New Jersey lost its first 18 games in 2009–10, setting a record for the worst start to an NBA season.

LEFT-HAND DRIVE

On January 30, 1977, the Nets trotted out a starting lineup of Al Skinner, Dave Wohl, Bubbles Hawkins, Kim Hughes, and Tim Bassett. All five players were left-handed. It was the first time in NBA history a team started five left-handed players. The lineup didn't pan out, as the Nets lost 100–92 to the Milwaukee Bucks.

RECORD SCOREKEEPER

Herb Turetzky was the franchise's official scorer for 54 years before retiring in 2021. He worked more than 2,200 games, starting with the first season in New Jersey. That record was certified by Guinness as the most professional basketball games scored.

GLOSSARY

assist
A pass that leads directly to a basket.

debut
To make a first appearance.

double-double
Accumulating 10 or more of two certain statistics in a game.

draft
A system that allows teams to acquire new players coming into a league.

era
A period of time in history.

forfeit
To lose a game without playing due to a broken rule or some other error.

free agent
A player whose rights are not owned by any team.

rookie
A professional athlete in his or her first year of competition.

triple-double
Accumulating 10 or more of three certain statistics in a game.

upset
An unexpected victory by a supposedly weaker team or player.

veteran
A player who has played many years.

MORE
INFORMATION

BOOKS

Flynn, Brendan. *The NBA Encyclopedia for Kids*. Minneapolis, MN: Abdo Publishing, 2022.

Mahoney, Brian. *GOATs of Basketball*. Minneapolis, MN: Abdo Publishing, 2022.

Ybarra, Andres. *Great Basketball Debates*. Minneapolis, MN: Abdo Publishing, 2019.

ONLINE RESOURCES

To learn more about the Brooklyn Nets, please visit **abdobooklinks.com** or scan this QR code. These links are routinely monitored and updated to provide the most current information available.

INDEX

ABOUT THE AUTHOR

Brian Mahoney has been a national NBA writer for the Associated Press since 2005, covering the NBA Finals, All-Star Games, and international basketball events such as the Olympics and basketball world championships. Based in New York, Mahoney covers the Knicks and Nets, along with providing coverage of boxing and tennis events. He is a 1995 graduate of the University of Connecticut, where he started his career covering the women's basketball team that won the national championship.